HOW TO COMMUNICATE WITH YOUR KIDS:
Keys to a Healthier, Happier Relationship with Your Kids

Shelley Harrison

Table of content

Chapter 1:

Introduction

When speaking to kids, it might sometimes seem as if all of your words are heard in one ear and not the other. You may get frustrated and the young people in your life may become disappointed if you are unable to connect and communicate with them. The development of a strong connection between you and your kid depends on open communication, which will also make it simpler for you to discuss challenging subjects with them when they become older. This book is for anybody who wants to encourage their children to put down their technology, improve their social skills, and form lifetime bonds via very interesting talks.

It will demonstrate how to interact with your children and support their socialization.

With that in mind, the goal of this book is to teach you how to communicate effectively with your children to help you build healthy connections with them.

Chapter 2:

Connecting with your kids

Talking to your kids is the simplest approach to establishing a connection with them. And you need to earn their trust if you want them to open up.

Every kid and parent has communication difficulties at some time. Some children seem to have an almost limitless capacity for communicating their needs, sharing their stories, and interacting with people around them. They can interact and connect because of their actions and their interpersonal and verbal communication styles. Other kids, on the other hand, could seem unresponsive, preoccupied, withdrawn, inattentive, or even shut down. So what can parents do to encourage conversation and support their kids' communication skills development?

It is common for kids to alternate between being more and less attentive. They need to put space between themselves at times. This does not imply that the separation will become irreversible. If they are given time to think independently before connecting again, they are more likely to desire to do so. Try your best not to take it personally if your kid asks for or demands this developmentally appropriate space from you, even if it's aimed at you. Give them some room to be quiet, think about their thoughts before expressing them, and find the right words to convey their experiences. A lot of effective communication involves being patient and empathic. Recognize that they are still developing their voice and that it will take time and patience on both your and their parts for them to do so.

Having said that, there are a few particular ways you may demonstrate that you are there to support them in speaking their minds and that you are interested in their experiences. These are techniques for letting people know you are trustworthy.
Practice listening and not overreacting.

Children often claim they avoid talking to their parents out of concern that they would make the situation worse. When they're a little older and you've shown them you can support them without losing your cool when they're being bullied on the playground, you'll hear about the lads in their group stealing. How are you going to keep yourself from entering? Breathe when your kid says something that makes you uncomfortable. Listen. Before you even start to speak, gather your composure.

When you do talk, hold off on offering suggestions. Assume that your kid will have clear ideas on how to resolve this issue and, with your assistance, can come up with a few alternatives.

Coach, hold back from running to your aid. (And sure, you may need to take more direct action if the issue persists. However, not the majority of the time, and not until you've encouraged your kid to attempt to manage the matter on his own.

Keep their secrets.

Do you recall how uncomfortable you were when your father casually said that you were afraid of spiders in front of the family? Or maybe your mother got in touch with the neighbors to let them know what you had informed her about their daughter? Everything your children tell you should be treated as private information. Speak to your kid first if you feel the need to share it with anybody else for any reason, even your spouse.

Tell the reality.

Make it a practice not to tell your kids white lies. Telling your youngster that the injection at the doctor's office won't hurt is alluring. But after that, why should she believe you? Be trustworthy from the beginning if you want to develop a trusting connection with your kid.

Pay attention to the phrases they avoid using.
Hearing is one thing, but listening is another; listening is an activity. Understanding a child's words is critical, but seeking to fully comprehend the child's underlying message is even more crucial. For instance, a youngster who cries, "I hate you, Mommy!" isn't expressing that; rather, she's more likely to be saying, "I'm angry because you're sending me to daycare instead of spending the day with me."

By repeating their statements back to them while focusing on emotional words, we may demonstrate to them that we are paying attention. "Are you saying you're upset because we have to be apart? I have to admit that I find it difficult to be apart from you. You also?" (Pause) "Let's find out a method to miss each other less throughout the day when I see you after circle time." (Bridge attachment)

By anticipating your child's needs based on verbal and nonverbal signs, Attune Attuning deepens listening. Knowing that a tantrum-prone youngster, for instance, really needs to sleep allows you to concentrate on soothing him or her rather than punishing them for acting out. The goal is to get the child horizontal.

Maintain eye contact

By concentrating on someone's eyes, one might understand a lot about their intentions. Get down and carefully gaze into a child's eyes while chatting to them. Show honesty to your kid by modeling it for them. Connecting is crucial and secure.

Respond

As long as they have faith that their cries for assistance will be heard, children will naturally seek assistance vocally or nonverbally. Your utmost effort should be put into responding to your child's pleas for assistance to foster trust and maintain their openness.

Aside from that, provide encouragement and affirmation to those who express emotion. Use phrases to demonstrate that you would keep your kid safe when they remark, "I'm terrified," such as, "I can see why you'd be afraid of the dark. Let's come up with a plan to assist you with that.

Do not invalidate by saying anything like, "Oh, monsters aren't real. You're experiencing unnecessary fear. A negative core belief such as "My emotions are wrong" (which they aren't) might unintentionally develop as a result.

Keep your word.
When you promise to do something for your kid, do it. Maintaining your word is not using it as an excuse to avoid responsibility or as an alternative to saying "no." Promise

just what is acceptable and feasible for you to carry out (relaxed). Be dependable.

Establish parameters, consistency, and a schedule

If you're asking how trust is affected, it is very significantly affected. The brain may unwind and get out of fight-or-flight mode when a youngster can trust that events will take place in a certain sequence.

Consistency and routines also lessen conflict because they prevent the youngster from succumbing to futility too quickly. For instance, if you calmly respond to a kid's request for "ten more minutes" by saying, "It would be wonderful to have ten more minutes, but it would put us in the late zone," the youngster is more likely to stop complaining. It's time for us to put our boots on after this song. (In this instruction, I utilized a scheduling cue, when/then, and transition signal.)

Consistency also lessens "crazy-making" because when someone anticipates a certain reaction, they might develop a feeling of justice in it. We may let our guard down when we believe we are being treated fairly.

A somewhat different form of trust—a firm conviction that a parent will protect safety and integrity—is developed via the establishment and enforcement of limits. When you establish a boundary, such as "No hitting," some kids may object. However, as they become older and realize that you are also protecting them from being harmed by others, they will respect your firmness.

Being honest about our flaws, worries, and difficulties fosters our children's confidence that doing so is safe. Giving your youngster knowledge teaches him or her how to do the same. Discuss appropriate ways to communicate information with others outside of your family as you go along. Don't overshare to avoid putting yourself in danger of predatory behavior on the part of others.

My sentiments are safe to express, so I will. We don't have to aim to be flawless; mistakes are OK.

You are not alone if you did not have a solid foundation of trust growing up. I am aware that it might be challenging to instill a sense of trust in your children when you find it difficult to do so yourself.

Communication between you and your kid will be simple after you've earned their trust.

Chapter 3:

Communicating with your kids

It's crucial to choose the appropriate phrases while speaking to children. You don't want your youngster to shut down and respond to you in a monosyllabic manner.

For instance, you may want to think about additional questions that would better encourage your child's openness before you initiate the discussion with the very natural, "How was your day?" If you don't, you could just get a one-word response like "good," "fine," or "boring."

The following inquiries may be used in place of "How was your day?"

- What was the highlight of the day for you?
- What task did you find most challenging today?
- Who would you choose as your three closest buddies to play or hang out with, and why?
- Who made you grin today, exactly?

- What was the day's least appealing aspect?
- What hue, and why, would you choose to represent today?
- What one original thing did you do today?
- Describe a book you're currently reading.
- Did you feel bored today? If not, why not?
- Describe a challenge you overcame today.
- Was it a fast or a leisurely day today? Why?
- What absurd rule are you supposed to follow?
- Has something occurred today that you are proud of?
- Have you encountered any specific difficulties today?
- What did you do today that was the most charitable?
- Do you want to ask me anything about your day?

- What are you now passionate about?
- What would you put in your lunch tomorrow if you could, and why?
- What did you discover today that you feel is the most significant?

The tone and strategies you use while speaking to young people may be heavily influenced by their age and stage of development. There is no one way to talk to kids, but with some helpful hints and techniques, everyone may find the conversation more entertaining and meaningful.

With young children, it's crucial to provide an example of good communication methods and tactics. When speaking to your children, remember to go at their pace, pay attention to their developmental stage, and make the dialogue as upbeat as you can!

When speaking to children, use their names. It focuses their attention on your voice and alerts them to what you are going to say while you are speaking to your children.

When speaking to kids, using their name creates a warm and cordial atmosphere.

Wait until you have a small child's complete attention before starting a conversation. Before you start talking to them, give them a moment to complete what they are doing and establish eye contact with you. They won't understand much of what you say if you don't do this.

Work to include uplifting words and phrases.
Maintaining a cheerful attitude when speaking is essential for establishing linguistic rapport with both young and older children. Substitute positive words and phrases with negative ones. Examples include

- Rather than yelling, "Don't run!" Say "Walk, please."
- Substitute "Let's try to hold off until dinnertime!" for "No more snacks!"

- Say anything other than "Don't quarrel with your sister!" Say something like, "Let's try to solve this jointly.

With young toddlers, maintaining eye contact is a crucial tactic for fostering meaningful conversations. Keep your eyes open while speaking to small children, even if they don't. Keep in mind that kids will learn to communicate with others by watching you.

Conduct a tone check

How would you rate your tone of voice? Do you have a loud voice, talk rapidly, or act obnoxiously? When speaking to small children, these are not the ones you want to use. Keep your voice clear and calm. Avoid speaking too quickly, and limit conversational subjects to a minimum.

Give children several options while having discussions.

Always provide options in conversations with children. Everyone dislikes living under a dictatorship, even kids. Kids prefer to feel like they have some choice in their environment, even if you are technically the boss, making all the decisions and setting the rules. You may use options in conversations with children to help them feel like they have some control over their lives and to develop their independence and decision-making abilities. Offering alternatives can include:

We could ride our bikes or go for a stroll today.

Paint or playdough was your preference?

I'm aware that you like board games. Which game, Candy Land or Shoots and Ladders, sounds better?

Conversation starters for kids and tweens

Tell me about your day's highlights and lowlights.

What game do you like to play?

What animal, if any, would you like to be, and why?

Where would you be if you could be anyplace right now? Which action would you take?

Which cereal is your favorite? Why?

What is the funniest expression you can muster?

Which song is your favorite? Why are you fond of it?

Which of your past vacations was the best?

Where do you like travelling to with a car?

What would you want to purchase if we went to the supermarket?

How many zoo sounds can you produce?

Have you ever had a fictional companion? Describe him to me.

How much higher can you go?

What three wishes, if any, would you want to make?
What kind of weather do you prefer? Why are you a fan of the weather?
Since when did you last exclaim, "I do!"
Which of your creations is the coolest?
When did you last act foolishly? How did you act?
Which pizza, if any, would you want to be?
What do you want to accomplish in life?
What Saturdays do you enjoy best?
What do you find objectionable?
Tell me about your favorite film or television program.
Which toy would you retain if you could only keep one? Why?
Which book, if any, would you keep if you could only keep one? Why?
Which period of the day is your favorite? Why?
What was the finest present you have ever gotten? What set it apart?
What aspect of your family do you love the most?

What clothing do you like to wear? What aspects of it do you like?

What was the dream you found most intriguing?

What do you like most about your instructor?

What superpower, if any, would you like to have?

What time of day is your favorite?

Did you discover anything new today at school?

Which holiday is your favorite?

What is a happy memory of yours?

What do you consider to be the greatest thing about growing up?

What about being a child is the best?

What about being a child is the worst?

What is it about the world that you wish you could alter?

Which of the following genuinely frightens you?

Which animated character is your favorite, and why?

What do you suppose our pet would say if it could talk?
To whom did you play today at school?
What is the one thing you are most anticipating right now?
What would you do with a magic wand first if you had one?
What did you have today for lunch?
Which event or circumstance made you grin today?
Which regulations, if any, would you impose as a parent?

How to Interact with and Talk to Older Children

Speaking with young children and teens demands a different approach than conversing with older children and youngsters. Make emerging adults feel as if you are speaking to them, rather than at them, and be appreciative of this new period of life.

Don't Be Demeaning to Them

Older kids don't like being spoken down to. They want to be treated more like adults than children since they are developing quickly. When you talk to your kid:

Stay away from using cutesy nicknames.

Utilize open-ended inquiries

Don't speak in a sing-songy voice; speak clearly.

Never challenge their choices, particularly those of the younger ones.

Discover How to Listen

The strong views that older children and teenagers have about EVERYTHING might lead to a power struggle between parents and their developing children. Always remember to pause and listen when talks get tense or emotional. In every connection, including the one you have with your kid, it is crucial to listen well. Show them the value of listening well so they may become better listeners to others in their own lives.

Speaking and listening are both crucial conversational skills.

Discover How To Assess Your Reactions

There will be certain chats with your older children that will make you want to respond immediately. Keep in mind that children can easily read your emotions, so be aware of the ones you are showing. They may shut down if you get upset about anything they are disclosing. Before sharing your point of view, keep your emotions in check and give yourself time to think.

Know when to step away from a teenager's attitude to keep interactions fruitful and cheerful. There is no good coming from two shouting parties. Take calm breaths, resist being duped and keep in mind who the grownup in this situation is.

Be a sounding board and a voice of reason

Be aware of when your adolescent, older kid or even an adult child wants your opinions and ideas and when they need you to serve as a sounding board while you are speaking with them. Try your best to read the clues and be the discussion partner that your kid needs at the time. It might be difficult to decide if you need to be the voice of reason or a shoulder to cry on.

Verify Your Feelings

The tendency of older children and teenagers to have erratic emotions is well known. In addition, describing one's sentiments may be a challenging endeavor in and of itself. When your older kid expresses their sentiments to you, try to understand them.

Think about utilizing words like:

I can see why you could be displeased with (name of a friend).

You must have felt very uncomfortable throughout it. I regret that you had to experience it.

This seems to be a really difficult situation.

It seems like this breakup has been painful for you.

In the future, children will feel more at ease opening up to adults if their sentiments are more often acknowledged.

Pick a Good Time to Speak

Teenagers are prone to mood swings that occur suddenly. Then, all of a sudden, they start to act withdrawn, melancholy, and morose. It may be challenging for parents to determine when to talk to older children and teenagers due to mood swings. Consider carefully and thoughtfully when participating in important discussions.

Converse during meals. A terrific time for adults and older kids to discuss serious topics is over a shared dinner.

Try chatting to your adolescent on a long vehicle journey if you want to discuss a subject that they would ordinarily avoid.
Don't attempt to talk to someone in front of their friends or shortly before a big event in their life, such as an exam or a game.

Strong relationships are fostered through strong communication.
Create dependable, meaningful channels of contact with children while they are young. So that they may imitate your good communication and listening techniques and apply them to other interpersonal interactions. Think about how you speak to your kids and evaluate your tactics as they become older and mature. Communication styles will develop and evolve with children the same way they do. The most crucial advice when speaking to children is to simply never stop. When speaking with children, young and old, always keep the channels of communication open and place a strong emphasis on respect and trust.

Teen conversation starters

As children become older, they often consider how their lives could vary from the families of their peers or the families they see on television. Hearing their opinions on the aspects of your family that they value and those that they may wish were different might open your eyes.

Ask your youngster some follow-up questions instead of defending or debating the details of your family that may be a bit difficult to hear.

On the other side, finding out what your kid loves and values most about being a member of your family may surprise and honor you.

These inquiries about family may start intriguing discussions:

Do you consider our family's punishments and penalties to be just?

What would your three proposed family rules be?

What lessons from our lessons stand out to you the most?
What about your siblings do you enjoy best? or relatives (if your kid is an only child).
What do you consider to be the most crucial traits of a good parent?
What is your preferred family custom?
Which aspect of our family is your favorite?
What should our family do more of?

Here are some topics for dialogue that might foster gratitude:
What are some things we take for granted yet are genuinely fortunate to have? (For instance, although rainy days may thwart our goals, they also promote garden growth and provide water for animals.)
What are some things you like having now that I didn't have when you were a child?
What are some items you have that you don't need but are grateful for?
What are some things that you can perform that maybe other people aren't able to—or aren't permitted to—do?

What do you have cause for gratitude today? Raising a kid who is grateful for what they have requires asking questions that foster thankfulness.

These inventive discussion starters can encourage your youngster to use greater imagination:

What superpower, if any, would you like to have? How would you choose it?

What would you buy if you won $100?

What would the subject of your book be?

What would your dogs say if they could communicate?

Which shade do you consider to be the happiest? Why does it cause you to smile?

Here are some queries that might aid in your child's growth as an empath.

Have you had an opportunity today to show kindness to anyone?

What do you believe young people who make fun of others think of themselves? How do you suppose bullied children feel?

When you are nice to someone, how do you think they feel?
What one thing in the world would you alter if you could?
Who is made fun of in school? Why are they made fun of? Do people ever speak out when children are being teased?
Empathy-based parenting is particularly crucial for adolescents and young adults. They'll begin to regard others like they ought to.
The development of an emotionally intelligent child is equally crucial.

Here are some easy discussion starters that might aid children in developing mental toughness:
How do you go about overcoming your fears?
Which of the following emotions—embarrassment, rage, fear, or another—do you believe to be the most unsettling?

What are some things you may say to yourself to modify these beliefs when your brain causes you to believe them, such as "you'll never succeed" or "no one likes you?"

Here are a few discussion topics that might assist your kid think about and building their ethics to aid in the development of ethical thinking and morals:

Should the other kids share with your buddy if they forget to pack lunch?

Is it ever OK to cheat in sports or school?

Is there ever a situation when robbing someone would be acceptable?

Here are some topics for dialogue to help your kid feel more confident:

How can you alter the course of the world?

What do you most relish in?

What skill or talent do you have?

Here are some topics for discussion that might encourage your kid to consider the future and foster the desire to design the life they want and achieve their objectives:

What would you want to do if you could, despite how seemingly unattainable it may seem?
What do you want to accomplish in life?
What one goal do you have before you graduate from college?
Which city would you most want to reside in? a farm, a mansion, an apartment in the city, a home in the country, an RV that's always traveling, or someplace else?
Just ask one or two "big questions" each day. Spend some time discussing your child's ideas and opinions while also demonstrating your interest in what they have to say. When your kid sees that you respect their viewpoint, even when it differs from your own, they will enjoy your talks.

Naturally occurring inquiries and conversation openers are preferable to interrogative ones. Your youngster is more likely to get overwhelmed and shut down if you ask them a lot of questions in a short time.

www.ingramcontent.com/pod-product-compliance
Lightning Source LLC
LaVergne TN
LVHW020535160826
845677LV00015B/4077

* 9 7 9 8 8 4 5 8 2 2 5 6 7 *